Kenya Safari

by Grace Hansen

Abdo WORLD SAFARIS Kids

Abdo Kids Jumbo is an Imprint of Abdo Kids
abdobooks.com

abdobooks.com

Published by Abdo Kids, a division of ABDO, P.O. Box 398166, Minneapolis, Minnesota 55439.

Printed in the United States of America, North Mankato, Minnesota.

052024

092024

THIS BOOK CONTAINS RECYCLED MATERIALS

Photo Credits: Alamy, Getty Images, Shutterstock

Production Contributors: Teddy Borth, Jennie Forsberg, Grace Hansen
Design Contributors: Victoria Bates, Candice Keimig

Library of Congress Control Number: 2023948669

Publisher's Cataloging-in-Publication Data

Names: Hansen, Grace, author.

Title: Kenya safari / by Grace Hansen

Description: Minneapolis, Minnesota : Abdo Kids, 2025 | Series: World safaris | Includes online resources and index.

Identifiers: ISBN 9798384900832 (lib. bdg.) | ISBN 9798384901532 (ebook) | ISBN 9798384901884 (Read-to-me eBook)

Subjects: LCSH: Safaris--Juvenile literature. | Natural areas--Juvenile literature. | Kenya--Description and travel--Juvenile literature. | Wilderness areas--Juvenile literature. | Travel--Juvenile literature.

Classification: DDC 967.62--dc23

Table of Contents

Let's Go on Safari!

Kenya is a country in East Africa. It is home to some of Earth's most amazing animals. Let's go on safari in Kenya!

Africa
Kenya
Atlantic Ocean
Indian Ocean

A safari is a tour where people can see wild animals in their **habitats**. There are many ways to go on safari in Kenya. Some people go by foot or Jeep. Others might go by hot-air balloon!

Wildlife in Kenya

The hippopotamus is one of the most dangerous animals in the world. It lives throughout Kenya. It is often seen in or near lakes and rivers. Hippos stay in the water most of the day to keep cool.

The Nile crocodile is found in the same **habitats** as the hippo. It is Africa's largest freshwater **predator**. Nile crocodiles can grow up to 20 feet (6.1 m) long!

Wildebeest can be seen bravely crossing rivers during their massive **migration**. In August, Safari-goers can see about one million wildebeest in the **Masai Mara**. Moving with them are hundreds of thousands of zebras.

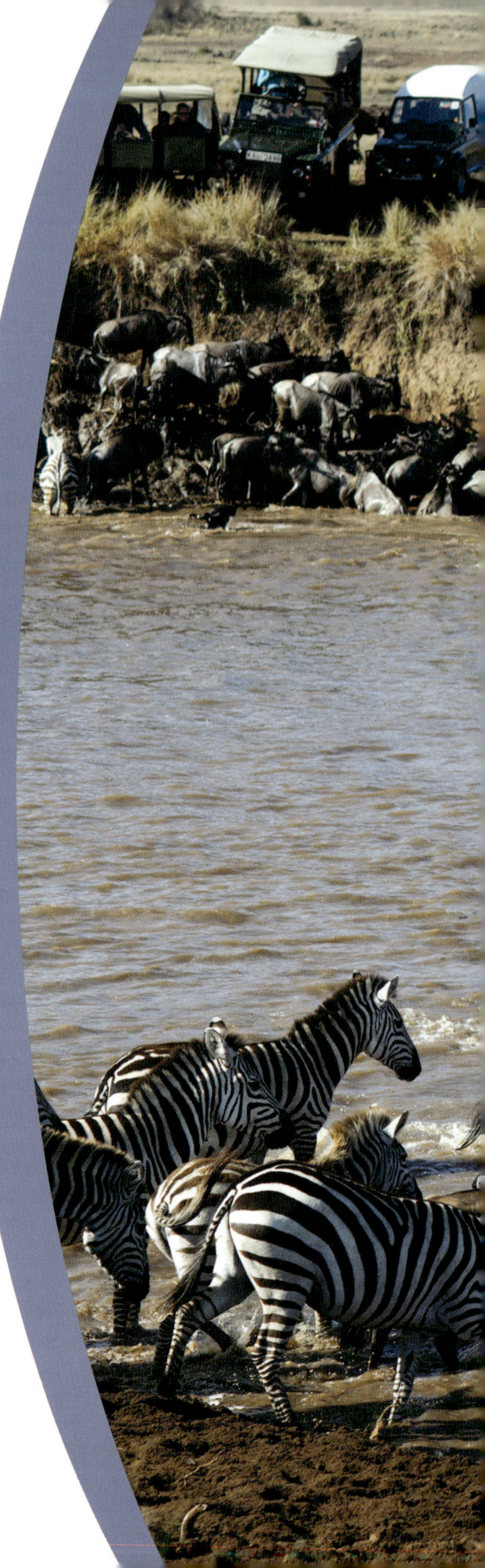

Cheetahs prefer wide-open spaces with few trees. This is where they do their best hunting. Cheetahs can be seen sitting on large **termite mounds**, searching for their next meal.

Masai ostriches live in the same **habitats** as cheetahs. They are some of the largest birds in the world. Only the North African ostrich is bigger.

Three **species** of giraffes are common throughout Kenya. The largest is the Masai giraffe. It is known for its unique leaf-like markings.

Groups of elephants and lions are both common sights on safari in Kenya. Elephants spend most of their days eating, drinking, and rolling in mud. Lions spend about 21 hours of the day resting.

Kenya Safari Experiences

Camel Safari
Walking safari with supplies carried by camels

Fly Camping
Walking safari and sleeping in a simple tent

Mobile Safari
Guided safari that moves locations day to day

Quad Bike Safari
Off-road safari on a four-wheeled power vehicle

Glossary

habitat – the natural environment of a plant or animal.

Masai Mara – a large wildlife reserve located in southwest Kenya.

migration – the act of moving from one place to another for food, water, or to have young.

predator – an animal that hunts other animals for food.

species – a group of living things that look alike and can have young together.

termite mound – a structure made of soil, termite saliva, and other materials that was made by termites. A termite is an insect that looks somewhat like an ant, lives in large groups, and eats wood.

Index